SIOUX

Sarah Tieck

www.abdopublishing.com

Published by Abdo Publishing, a division of ABDO, PO Box 398166, Minneapolis, Minnesota 55439.
Copyright © 2015 by Abdo Consulting Group, Inc. International copyrights reserved in all countries. No part
of this book may be reproduced in any form without written permission from the publisher. Big Buddy Books™
is a trademark and logo of Abdo Publishing.

Printed in the United States of America, North Mankato, Minnesota.
042014
092014

THIS BOOK CONTAINS
RECYCLED MATERIALS

Cover Photo: AARON HUEY/National Geographic Creative.
Interior Photos: Getty Images (pp. 5, 25, 27, 29, 30); Glow Images (p. 19); © Nancy G Western Photography, Nancy
    Greifenhagen/Alamy (p. 11); © NativeStock.com/AngelWynn (pp. 15, 16, 17, 25); © North Wind/Nancy Carter/
    North Wind Picture Archives (p. 9); ©Pictorial Press Ltd/Alamy (p. 15); Shutterstock (pp. 13, 21, 23, 26).

Coordinating Series Editor: Rochelle Baltzer
Contributing Editors: Megan M. Gunderson, Marcia Zappa
Graphic Design: Adam Craven

Library of Congress Cataloging-in-Publication Data

Tieck, Sarah, 1976-
  Sioux / Sarah Tieck.
     pages cm. -- (Native Americans)
  ISBN 978-1-62403-357-5
1. Dakota Indians--History--Juvenile literature. 2. Dakota Indians--Social life and customs--Juvenile literature. I.
Title.
  E99.D1T54 2014
  978.004'975243--dc23
                        2014001422

CONTENTS

Amazing People

Hundreds of years ago, North America was mostly wild, open land. Native Americans lived on the land. They had their own languages and **customs**.

The Sioux (SOO) are one Native American nation. They are known for their brave fighters and strong leaders. Let's learn more about these Native Americans.

Did You Know?

Some say the name *Sioux* means "enemies." It may have been given to the nation by the Ojibwa people.

Today, the Sioux people keep a connection to their past and their homelands.

Sioux Territory

The Sioux nation lived in parts of present-day Minnesota, North Dakota, South Dakota, Montana, Nebraska, Iowa, and Wisconsin. Some people also lived in Canada.

The Sioux lived on the plains. The people hunted and farmed on the grassy land. They used water from nearby lakes and rivers.

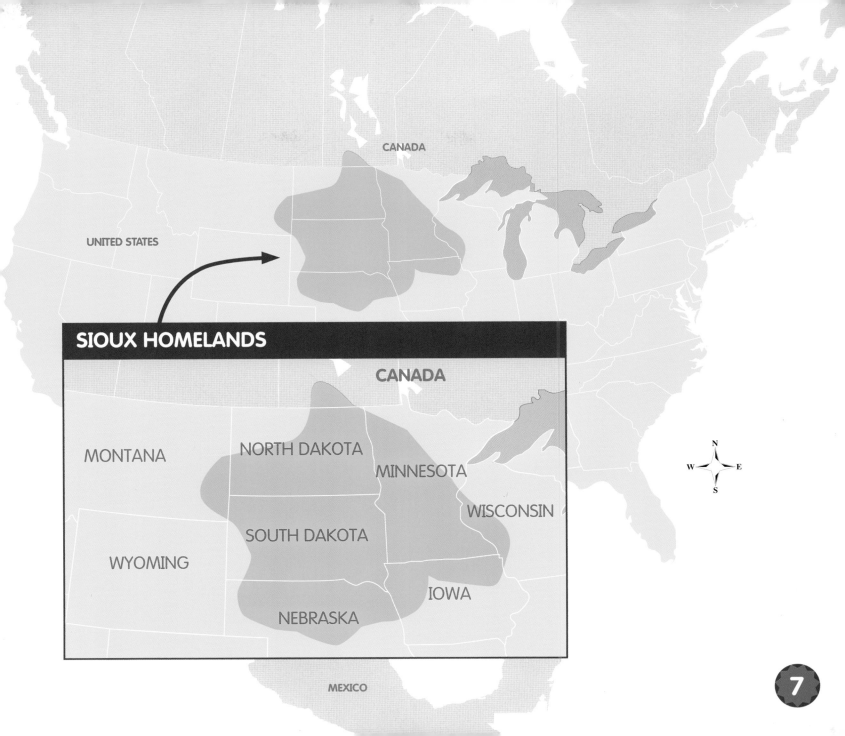

CANADA

UNITED STATES

SIOUX HOMELANDS

CANADA

MONTANA

NORTH DAKOTA

MINNESOTA

WISCONSIN

SOUTH DAKOTA

WYOMING

IOWA

NEBRASKA

MEXICO

N
W E
S

HOME LIFE

Most Sioux lived in homes called teepees. These were easy to set up and move. Teepees were made of strong wooden poles and buffalo skins. The women skinned buffalo and prepared the skin to cover their homes.

The Sioux built a small fire in the center of each teepee. People used it to cook and keep warm. Smoke escaped through a hole in the top. When it rained or snowed, people closed the hole with a piece of buffalo skin.

Did You Know?

Children had very small teepees to play with or use as dollhouses.

The men often painted the outside of teepees. They drew pictures that had special meaning to them.

What They Ate

The Sioux were mainly hunters and gatherers. They were **nomads**. So, they moved around in search of food. They hunted animals such as deer and buffalo. They also caught fish.

The Sioux gathered fruits, vegetables, and grains from the land. These included berries and wild rice. Sometimes, tribes traded with each other for food.

The Sioux often used bows and arrows to hunt.

The American bison, or buffalo, was an important food source for the Sioux. Boys learned to hunt at a young age. Often, they would ride horses and carry bows and arrows.

Buffalo had many uses. The tribe used the skins for clothing and shelter. The meat was a key source of food. When the hunters came home, the women would turn the meat into jerky. First, they cut it into strips. Then, they dried it.

Did You Know?

Today, there are only about 20,000 buffalo roaming the plains. But, before Europeans arrived, there were about 50 million!

Have you ever tried eating jerky? This dried food kept for a long time without going bad. It was also easy for hunters to carry with them.

A full-grown male buffalo can be more than ten feet (3 m) long. It can weigh around 2,000 pounds (900 kg)!

DAILY LIFE

The Sioux were a huge nation of people spread across the plains. There were many tribes split into three main groups. The groups were the Santee, Yankton, and Teton.

Many Sioux lived in camps. Within the camps, people had different jobs. The men hunted and fought in wars. Some became medicine men or chiefs. The women cooked meals and ran the camps.

Did You Know?

Medicine men were important to the Sioux. They were spiritual leaders and healers.

Sitting Bull was a Teton Sioux chief and a medicine man. He helped his people prepare for battles, such as the Battle of the Little Bighorn. He died in 1890.

Crazy Horse was a Teton Sioux leader. He helped his people fight for their land. He was known for his bravery and his ideas. He fought at the Battle of the Little Bighorn. He died in 1877.

Made by Hand

The Sioux made their own food, clothes, and tools. They gathered firewood and pounded jerky. They decorated with beads and porcupine quills.

Personal Items

The Sioux wore necklaces, earrings, arm bands, and bags. These were made of shells, bones, and beads. The bravest men wore bear claws!

Star Quilts

The Sioux made quilts sewn together in the shape of a star. These were often given as special gifts for important events.

Buffalo Robes

The Sioux often wrapped themselves in buffalo furs to stay warm. They tried to use everything they could from animals they hunted.

Dressed in Animal Skins

Women wore deerskin or buffalo skin dresses. Men wore leggings and sometimes shirts. The Sioux often decorated their clothes and moccasins with colorful beads.

Spirit Life

Religion was important to the Sioux way of life. The people believed plants, animals, and all things have power. If they behaved well, this power helped them. If they behaved badly, it hurt them.

Sioux medicine men led tribe members in special dances and **ceremonies**. People also smoked pipes and shared their dreams and visions. They believed these were ways to talk to powerful beings.

The Sun Dance is often shown in Sioux art.
It took place in late spring or early summer.

STORYTELLERS

The Sioux people told stories. Sometimes they drew stories using **symbols**. These folktales and myths taught people history and lessons. But some simply entertained them. Storytelling was a way to pass on ideas and beliefs to new **generations**.

Coyote and Iktomi are important characters in Sioux stories. They are often tricksters. *Iktomi* means "spider."

Fighting for Land

Land was very important to the Sioux. Places such as the Black Hills were considered **sacred**. Important tribe stories and leaders are connected to this land, also known as *Paha Sapa*.

In 1868, the US government and the Sioux signed papers at Fort Laramie. They said the Sioux owned the Black Hills. Gold was discovered there in the 1870s. After that, American settlers began to travel to the land.

The Black Hills are small mountains in South Dakota and Wyoming.

Settlers killed more buffalo than they needed. They took gold and other **resources**. The US government told the Sioux to live on **reservations**. There, they tried to farm, but many people struggled.

Over the years, the Sioux and the settlers battled over land. In 1876, the Sioux famously fought in the Battle of the Little Bighorn. And, there were two armed fights at Wounded Knee in South Dakota. Today, the Sioux work to gain back land that was taken from them.

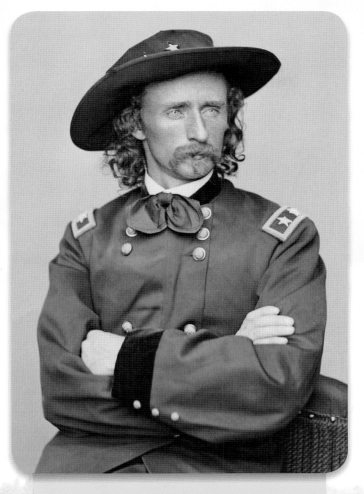

US Lieutenant Colonel George Custer and his soldiers fought the Sioux in the Battle of the Little Bighorn. Custer and his men died. So, it is also called "Custer's Last Stand."

The more than 200 Sioux people who died at Wounded Knee in 1890 are remembered today. They were killed by US soldiers who feared they would start an uprising.

Back in Time

About 1831

Sitting Bull was born. He was a famous medicine man and Sioux leader. He is remembered for his great bravery.

1600s

Horses became common on the plains. This made it easier for tribe members to carry objects, move around, and hunt.

1876

Sioux warriors fought and won against US Army troops led by Lieutenant Colonel George Custer. This became known as the Battle of the Little Bighorn, or "Custer's Last Stand."

1948

In the Black Hills, construction started on a giant sculpture of Crazy Horse. Much of it is still unfinished. But, Crazy Horse's completed head is nearly 90 feet (27 m) tall!

1890

More than 200 Sioux people died in the Battle of Wounded Knee.

1973

About 200 Native Americans held a **protest** at Wounded Knee in South Dakota. Members of the American Indian Movement took control for 71 days. They wanted a new leader and better treatment from the US government.

A Strong Nation

The Sioux people have a long, rich history. They are remembered for their teepees and buffalo hunting skills. They are also known for strong leaders, such as Sitting Bull and Crazy Horse.

Sioux roots run deep. Today, the people have kept alive those special things that make them Sioux. Even though times have changed, many people carry the **traditions**, stories, and memories of the past into the present.

Did You Know?

Today, there are about 113,000 Sioux living in the United States.

Traditional clothing is an important part of some tribal events.

"Let us put our minds together and see what life we can make for our children."

— Sitting Bull

GLOSSARY

ceremony a formal event on a special occasion.
custom a practice that has been around a long time and is common to a group or a place.
generation (jeh-nuh-RAY-shuhn) a single step in the history of a family.
nomads people that travel from place to place.
protest an event where people speak out against or object to something.
reservation (reh-zuhr-VAY-shuhn) a piece of land set aside by the government for Native Americans to live on.
resource a supply of something useful or valued.
sacred (SAY-kruhd) connected with worship of a god.
symbol (SIHM-buhl) an object or mark that stands for an idea.
tradition (truh-DIH-shuhn) a belief, a custom, or a story handed down from older people to younger people.

WEBSITES

To learn more about Native Americans, visit **booklinks.abdopublishing.com**. These links are routinely monitored and updated to provide the most current information available.

INDEX